Jazz Violin Studies

A Complete Study & Reference Book

By Usher Abell

Online Audio   www.melbay.com/93954BCDEB

Audio Contents

<blockquote>
[1] Introduction: Jazz Violin Study #54 (pg. 55) [2:08]
</blockquote>

1 Introduction: Jazz Violin Study #54 (pg. 55) [2:08]	The Slide-Exercise #7 (pg. 31) [:22]	50 Chords-Exercise #39 (pg. 47) [:15]
2 Introduction [:34]	Chords-Exercise #1 (pg. 39) [:45]	51 Chords-Exercise #40 (pg. 47) [:15]
3 Tuning [:14]	Chords-Exercise #3 (pg. 39) [:23]	52 Chords-Exercise #41 (pg. 47) [:16]
4 Style-Exercise #2 (pg. 9) [:38]	Chords-Exercise #4 (pg. 39) [:12]	53 Chords-Exercise #44 (pg. 49) [1:05]
5 Style-Exercise #3 (pg. 9) [:36]	Chords-Exercise #5 (pg. 40) [:13]	54 Chords-Exercise #46 (pg. 50) [:25]
6 Style-Exercise #4 (pg. 9) [:36]	Chords-Exercise #8 (pg. 40) [:19]	55 Chords-Exercise #48 (pg. 51) [:36]
7 Style-Exercise #5 (pg. 10) [:17]	Chords-Exercise #9 (pg. 41) [:23]	56 Chords-Exercise #53 (pg. 54) [2:55]
8 Style-Exercise #6 (pg. 10) [:42]	Chords-Exercise #10 (pg. 41) [:19]	57 Diminished Seventh Chords-Exercise #1 (pg. 58) [:18]
9 Style-Exercise #7 (pg. 10) [:25]	Chords-Exercise #14 (pg. 42) [:14]	58 Diminished Seventh Chords-Exercise #2 (pg. 58) [:18]
10 Style-Exercise #8 (pg. 10) [:24]	Chords-Exercise #15 (pg. 42) [:14]	59 Diminished Seventh Chords-Exercise #3 (pg. 58) [:23]
11 Style-Exercise #9 (pg. 11) [:26]	Chords-Exercise #16 (pg. 42) [:22]	60 Careless Love (pg. 92) [1:27]
12 Style-Exercise #10 (pg. 11) [:25]	Chords-Exercise #17 (pg. 43) [:25]	61 Every Night When the Sun Goes In (pg. 95) [2:11]
13 Seventh Chord Sequences-Exercise #13 (pg. 12) [1:09]	Chords-Exercise #19 (pg. 43) [:15]	62 Sweet and Sour & Sweet and Sour Jam (pg. 98) [4:23]
14 Syncopation-Exercise #5 (pg. 20) [:21]	Chords-Exercise #20 (pg. 43) [:12]	63 Sixteen Jazz Violin Pieces and Studies-Exercise 2 (pg. 104) [3:00
15 Syncopation-Exercise #6 (pg. 20) [:24]	Chords-Exercise #21 (pg. 44) [:15]	64 Sixteen Jazz Violin Pieces and Studies-Exercise 6 (pg. 106) [1:24
16 Syncopation-Exercise #7 (pg. 20) [:14]	Chords-Exercise #22 (pg. 44) [:13]	65 Sixteen Jazz Violin Pieces and Studies-Exercise 9 (pg. 108) [2:04
17 Syncopation-Exercise #8 (pg. 20) [:14]	Chords-Exercise #23 (pg. 44) [:15]	66 Sixteen Jazz Violin Pieces and Studies-Exercise 13 (pg. 111) [3:2
18 Syncopation-Exercise #9 (pg. 20) [:29]	Chords-Exercise #24 (pg. 44) [:14]	67 Sixteen Jazz Violin Pieces and Studies-Exercise 14 (pg. 112) [2:0
19 Syncopation-Exercise #10 (pg. 21) [:33]	Chords-Exercise #25 (pg. 44) [:15]	68 Sixteen Jazz Violin Pieces and Studies-Exercise 16 (pg. 113) [1:3
20 Syncopation-Exercise #12 (pg. 21) [:38]	Chords-Exercise #31 (pg. 46) [:22]	69 Oh, When the Saints Go Marching In (pg. 116) [1:31]
21 Syncopation-Exercise #13 (pg. 22) [:40]	Chords-Exercise #32 (pg. 46) [:13]	70 Just a Closer Walk with Thee (pg. 122) [2:57]
22 Syncopation-Exercise #14 (pg. 22) [:41]	Chords-Exercise #33 (pg. 46) [:15]	71 Fiddler's Folly (pg. 137) [2:09]
23 The Slide-Exercise #3 (pg. 30) [:38]	Chords-Exercise #35 (pg. 46) [:15]	72 Sequel (pg. 143) [1:33]
24 The Slide-Exercise #4 (pg. 30) [:16]	Chords-Exercise #38 (pg. 47) [:17]	73 Wild Bird (pg. 148) [1:51]
25 The Slide-Exercise #6 (pg. 31) [:55]		

1 2 3 4 5 6 7 8 9 0

USHER ABELL

Usher Abell, violinist, is a native of Paducah, Kentucky, where he learned the jazz style at an early age. He continued to play with dance bands while studying for his music degrees and during World War II while serving as a musician in the Navy.

Mr. Abell served as a college music teacher and administrator for over thirty five years. He conducted the University of South Dakota Orchestra, taught strings and courses in arranging and orchestration. He was active as a performer in recitals, small ensembles and symphonies. Now retired from the University of South Dakota as a teacher, he is in demand as a jazz violin soloist with area groups.

During his many years of teaching Mr. Abell often had students who were interested in learning to play jazz and it was then that he realized the need for information which would assist the violinist who wanted to learn jazz techniques.

CONTENTS

INTRODUCTION

The purposes of the Jazz Violin Studies are to give the violinist (also applicable to the violist or 'cellist) experience in playing jazz, practice in the bowings and rhythmic styles used in jazz with "licks" of various lengths, based on a variety of types of chords.

It is assumed that the string player has a background on his instrument enabling him, or her, to play in tune, to perform with a good tone, and to possess, or acquire, an adequate technique.

A knowledge of basic harmony is necessary. If the string player has not had formal training in music theory or harmony help may be obtained from various music fundamentals books, theory books, and harmony books. Also, some collections of popular music include charts illustrating chord construction. A chart of some commonly used chords is included with these exercises.

It is the intent of the author that these exercises will furnish the string player 1) a practical approach to playing jazz on the violin, 2) an aid for developing his own ability to improvise, and 3) an approach for writing his own jazz arrangements.

JAZZ STYLES

Styles in playing jazz have undergone several changes during this century. Ragtime and the blues, predecessors of jazz, were characteristic of the period from around 1900 to 1920. During the period from about 1920 to 1930 we had the development of Dixieland and the early big bands of Duke Ellington and Fletcher Henderson. During this period Joe Venuti, violin, and Eddie Lang, guitar, began playing jazz and making recordings. Venuti's influence on jazz violin performance has been very great on many fiddlers, including Stephane Grappelli, and a host of others such as western swing and bluegrass players.

The 1930's saw the development of many big bands and of many outstanding jazz soloists. This period is known as the swing era. The swinging manner of playing eighth notes was characteristic of this era and continues to be used in most jazz styles. It was followed by the bebop era. The music of it is characterised by rapid chord changes, frequent modulations to other keys and a more vertical structure, as opposed to horizontal structure (scalewise), and the frequent use of two eighth notes slurred from the afterbeat to the strong beat ( ). Many examples of this bowing style are included in this book. Violinists who have often used this bebop style include Grappelli and Jean-Luc Ponty.

The 1950's, following the bebop era, saw a reaction to the bebop style develop. Tunes with fewer chord changes were used, sometimes employing a single chord for 8 to 16 measures. More use of the modal scales was made, especially the Dorian mode. If built on D it would contain the tones DEFGABCD. In other words, the half steps would occur between tones 2 (1 2 3 4 5 6 7 8) and 3 (E and F), and between 6 and 7 (B and C). In the 1960's we saw the development of free form tunes, further use of the modes, and the use of electronic devices .Jazz violinists Ponty, Urbaniak, and Pointer are examples of players who use electronic sounds. Most jazz and bluegrass fiddlers use amplified instruments.

Examples of the basic blues pattern are included, one in the chapter on Syncopation, and the tune "Every Night When the Sun Goes In," in the chapter on Variations. Characteristic of the blues style are the lowered third, fifth, and seventh tones of the scale. In the C scale the lowered notes would be E♭, G♭ and B♭. The chordal patterns in these examples are the simple traditional ones, but there are many other harmonic patterns commonly used in the blues. Also, many different tempos are used.

Many of the examples in the chapter on Chords include the swing style, often using the bebop manner of slurring the eighth notes. Also, in the chapter on Chords, exercises 45, 46, 47, and 48 are examples of bebop harmonic changes and of bebop bowing style.

In the chapter on Special Effects is an arrangement of "Old Joe Clark" using bluegrass and swing styles. It is in the Mixolydian mode. Beginning the mode on A it has this pattern: ABC♯DEF♯GA. In this mode the half steps
(1 2 3 4 5 6 7 8)
are between tones 3 and 4 (C♯ and D), and between 6 and 7 (F♯ and G). There are only two chord changes in this version of "Old Joe Clark."

Chords are constructed from scales (or modes), and there are many of them. For example, each scale may be built on any one of the twelve chromatic tones: C, C♯, D, D♯, E, F, F♯, G, G♯, A, A♯ and B. Since eleven scales are listed here you would have 132 possible scales and hundreds of chords available. Remember: this is only a partial list.

MODES (OR SCALES)

Ionian (major scale)

Dorian

Phrygian

Lydian

Mixolydian

Aeolian (natural form of minor)

Locrian

Blues scale

Pentatonic scale

Whole tone scale

Diminished scale

(for practice)
Transpose each one whole step up

(⌐¬) The bracket indicates where the half steps occur

RHYTHMIC AND BOWING STYLES

Rhythmic and bowing styles are probably the first and most important elements to be learned in performing jazz. In the following exercises pairs of eighth notes are usually played as triplets (♪♪ = ♩ ♪), not often as even eighth notes, (except in very fast tempos and in Latin styles.) Not all jazz performers agree as to exactly how the eighth note figures should be played, but in any case they must *swing*. (Listen to the playing of Grappelli, Venuti, or other fine jazz musicians.) The values of note values other than eighth notes are usually played as written. These same exercises will also include a variety of types of bowings. Bowings of the same type, such as all slurred or all separate, may soon become very uninteresting.

In actual performance each player will need to decide for himself which bowings are best for a particular passage or composition. These exercises are to help develop facility in bowing and rhythmic style.

Exercise [1] illustrates (a) how a two measure passage of even eighth notes may be written, and (b) how the passage sounds when played in a jazz style.

In the remaining exercises throughout the book be certain that the written notes sound in a triplet (♪♪ = ♩ ♪) manner.

STYLE

B.

Use the Same Amount of Bow for Each Stroke

Seventh Chord Sequences
(repeated regular patterns)

12

13

14 **Slowly at first, then faster**

15

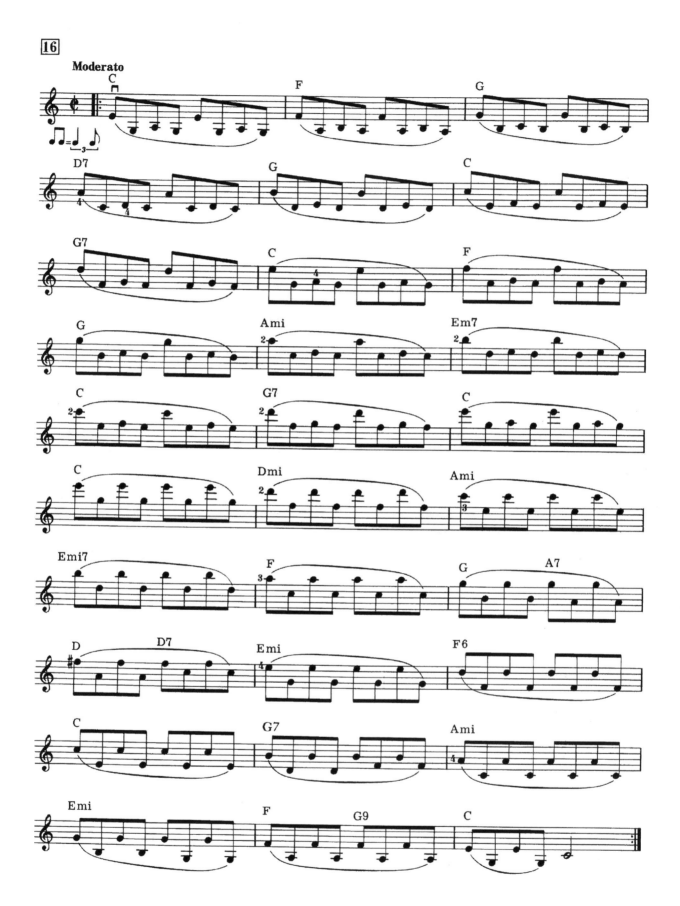

17

* Play loud passages at middle of bow
  Play soft passages in upper part of bow

18

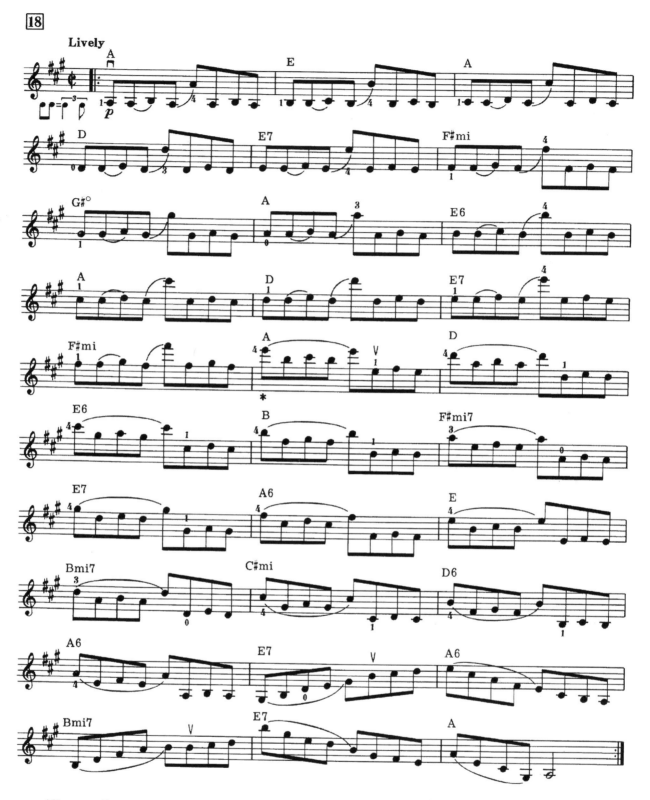

*Use small amount of bow for slurred notes. Practice entire study in both upper and lower parts of bow.

SYNCOPATION

One of the characteristics of jazz (and often used in many other types of music) is the use of syncopation, which may be defined as the shifting of the rhythmic accent from the strong beats of a measure to the weak, or unaccented, beats. (In 4/4 meter the weaker beats are two and four. Also, the last half of any beat is weaker that the first half.) See example [1]. In this example an asterisk (*) indicates the syncopated note.

Examples 2, 3 and 4 illustrate different methods of writing the same sounding exercise.

It is suggested that the remaining examples be played slowly and steadily at first, and then gradually increase the tempo.

The accents in the following exercises should be played very lightly.

* Indicates the syncopated note.

Syncopation Used in a Basic Blues Pattern

The accents should be very light.

BASIC BLUES

THE SLIDE OR PORTAMENTO

An important part of jazz string playing is the use of the slide, or portamento, into a note. It is indicated by a dash (╱) before the note. The dash (╲) is sometimes used following a note, in which case you slide the finger, or hand, downward, lowering the pitch, and using no vibrato.

It is suggested that the player start the slide a half step below the pitch and move into the principal tone rapidly. (See example 1). Example 2 illustrates how the slide is usually indicated, and it is suggested that the player practice this exercise until he does it to his own satisfaction. Eventually, each player must determine for himself how much to slide into a note and on which notes to use the slide.

The recordings of Venuti, Grappelli, and others, will illustrate how the leading jazz violinists use the slide.

This is a repetition of #14 in Syncopation, written a fifth higher, with suggested places to slide.

34

CHORDS

In jazz performance the melody and harmony are "centered" around certain chords. In improvisation, or in arrangements, the result may include only the chord tones of the particular music. Example $\boxed{1}$ in the section on chords illustrates this. Also, the music may include non-chord tones such as passing tones; neighboring tones; leaps; altered tones such as lowered thirds, fifths, or sevenths; chromatics, suspensions, and anticipations. (See the chart of non-chord tones.)

In the chord exercises some of the non-chord tones will be indicated by an X. The chord tones around which the exercises are based will be given at the beginning of some examples. Most of the exercises can be transposed to other keys. Several may be played a string higher, or a string lower.

The majority of the examples are given in 4/4 meter, and are indicated as slow, moderate, or lively. The final tempo will need to be determined by the individual player. It is suggested that most of the examples should be practised slowly at first.

The examples are of two or more measures in length. Since many of the standard tunes played in jazz are harmonized in two measure phrases, some of the examples are of that length. ' indicates the end of a phrase.

After the performer can play the exercises to his satisfaction he or she is encouraged to play them with either piano or guitar accompaniment.

The chart of non-chord tones and the chart of selected commonly used chords follow.

CHART OF NON-CHORD TONES

A.

( ) indicates the particular type of non-chord tone

SELECTED COMMONLY USED CHORDS

B.

Key		C	Cmi	C+	C6	Cmi6	C7	Cmi7	Cma7	C+7	C°	C9	C6/9	C7(b9)	C7(b5)
C															
D		D	Dmi	D+	D6	Dmi6	D7	Dmi7	Dma7	D+7	D°	D9	D6/9	D7(b9)	D7(b5)
Eb		Eb	Ebmi	Eb+	Eb6	Ebmi6	Eb7	Ebmi7	Ebma7	Eb+7	Eb°	Eb9	Eb6/9	Eb7(b9)	Eb7(b5)
E		E	Emi	E+	E6	Emi6	E7	Emi7	Ema7	E+7	E°	E9	E6/9	E7(b9)	E7(b5)
F		F	Fmi	F+	F6	Fmi6	F7	Fmi7	Fma7	F+7	F°	F9	F6/9	F7(b9)	F7(b5)
G		G	Gmi	G+	G6	Gmi6	G7	Gmi7	Gma7	G+7	G°	G9	G6/9	G7(b9)	G7(b5)
Ab		Ab	Abmi	Ab+	Ab6	Abmi6	Ab7	Abmi7	Abma7	Ab+7	Ab°	Ab9	Ab6/9	Ab7(b9)	Ab7(b5)
A		A	Ami	A+	A6	Ami6	A7	Ami7	Ama7	A+7	A°	A9	A6/9	A7(b9)	A7(b5)
Bb		Bb	Bbmi	Bb+	Bb6	Bbmi6	Bb7	Bbmi7	Bbma7	Bb+7	Bb°	Bb9	Bb6/9	Bb7(b9)	Bb7(b5)
B		B	Bmi	B+	B6	Bmi6	B7	Bmi7	Bma7	B+7	B°	B9	B6/9	B7(b9)	B7(b5)

CHORDS
(Phrases of two or more measures)

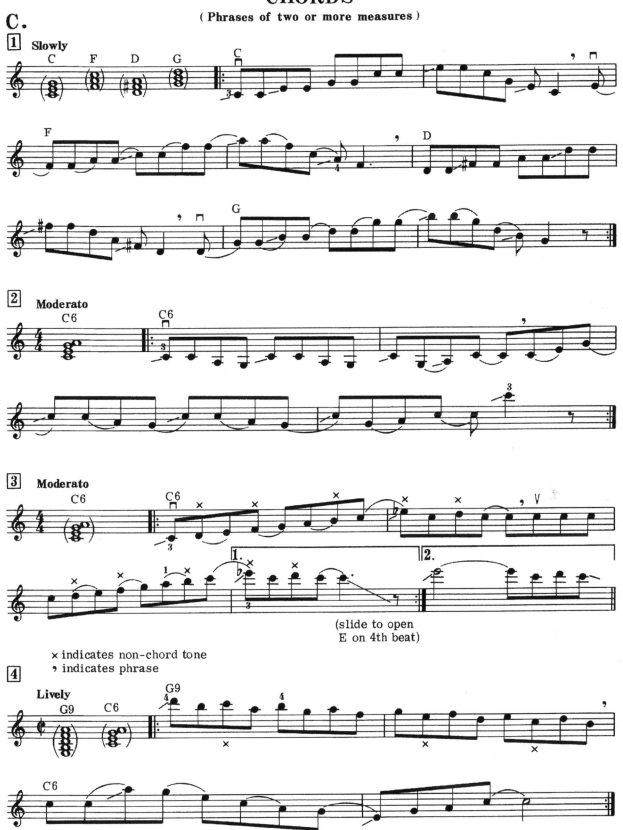

x indicates non-chord tone
, indicates phrase

(slide to open
E on 4th beat)

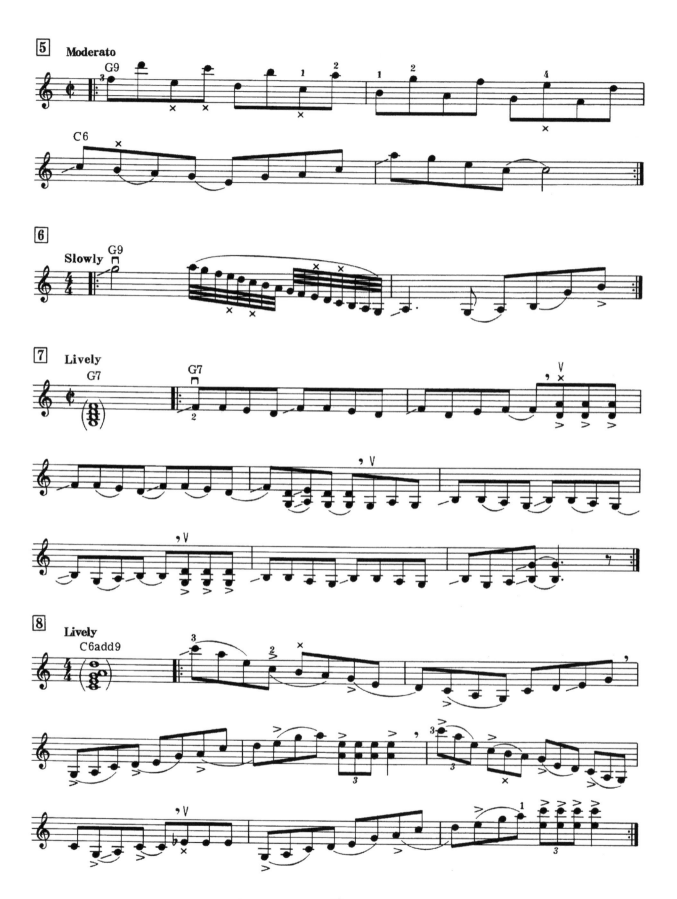

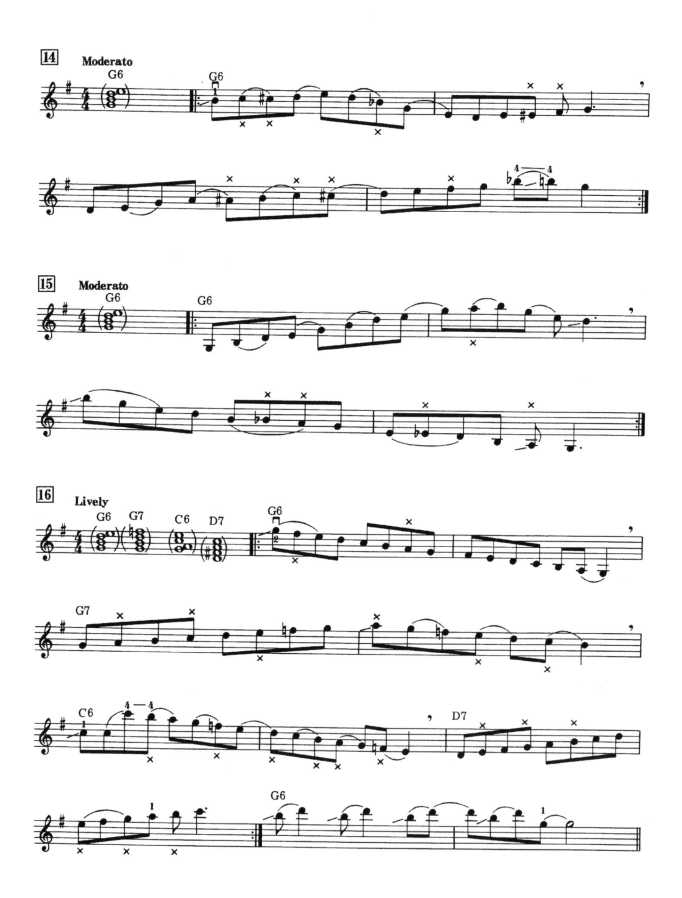

43

(fingered tremolo)

47

B♭6 (I 6) C7 (II7) F7 (V7) B♭6 (I 6) Progressions

Passages Using One or More Harmonic Changes in Each Measure

50

48

CHORDS TO #48

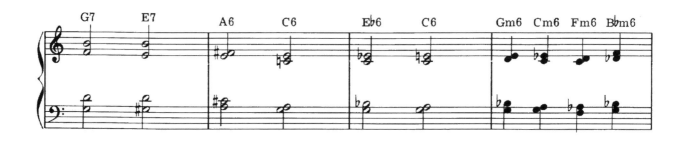

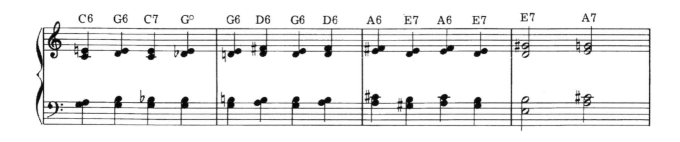

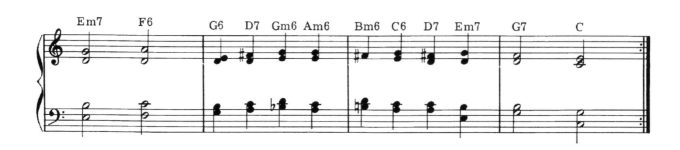

(sixth position)

DIMINISHED SEVENTH CHORDS

The diminished seventh chord is designated by a small circle (○), and is built with three minor thirds. For example, F♯° consists of F♯, A, C, E♭. The G♭° chord consists of G♭, B♭♭, D♭♭, F♭♭, and sounds the same as the F♯°; however, for convenience sake, the G♭ might be written G♭, A, C, E♭, or F♯, A, C, E♭. In other words, it has become common practice in popular music to use enharmonic substitutions (or spellings). Enharmonic means notes which have the same pitch, but a different name, i.e. F♯ and G♭ sound the same.

In actual sound there are only three diminished seventh chords, regardless of how they are spelled. (See the following examples.)

Examples of Diminished Seventh Chord Spellings

E

Examples 1-4-7-10 all sound the same
Examples 2-5-8-11 all sound the same
Examples 3-6-9-12 all sound the same

59

SPECIAL EFFECTS

Included in the chapter on "special effects" will be:

A. Harmonics

B. Double stops

C. Pizzicato

D. Arpeggio bowings

E. Tremolo bowings

F. Shuffle bowings

G. Staccato bowings

HARMONICS

Harmonics are "special effects" which are often used by string players. Jazz players, such as Grapelli, make much use of them. There are two types, natural and artificial.

The natural harmonics, for practical use, are produced by touching the open string lightly one octave higher, a twelfth higher, or two octaves higher. See exercise 1 . Natural harmonics sound where written and are indicated by a circle.

Artificial harmonics sound higher than written and are indicated by a diamond shaped note. The most common artificial harmonics are produced by lightly touching the string a perfect fourth higher, producing a sound two octaves higher than the bottom note. See example 2 .

Artificial harmonics can also be produced by lightly touching the string a perfect fifth higher, producing a sound a twelfth higher than the bottom note; or by touching the string a major sixth higher, producing a sound two octaves and a major third higher than the bottom note. These are the most practical ones. See example 3 .

1 (Natural)
sul G

Repeat this pattern on each string.

2
8va

(Sounding notes)
(Artificial)

(Written notes)

3 (Sounding)

8va

(3rd position)
D6

(Written)

4 Passages using artificial harmonies.

A

(3rd position)

5

D

6

G

* During the shift the finger must remain on the string.

62

PASSAGES USING NATURAL AND/OR ARTIFICIAL HARMONICS

A zero (0) indicates a natural harmonic (or an open string) and sounds the written pitch.

DOUBLE STOPS

The simplest double stops are those in the first position involving (1) open strings, (2) perfect fifths with the first and second fingers, (3) sixths with the first and second fingers, (4) minor sixths with the second and third fingers, (5) augmented fourths with the first and second fingers and with the second and third fingers, (6) and thirds with the first and third fingers. These finger patterns may be repeated a string higher or a string lower.

B.

Various examples of double stops.

67

PIZZICATO

There are two types of pizzicato, that which is plucked with the index finger of the right hand, indicated by pizz., and left hand pizzicato, indicated by a +. To return to using the bow arco is indicated.

C.

Pizzicato Blues

ARPEGGIO BOWING

More of the bowings used by classical string players are now being used by jazz players. The arpeggio bowing is one which may be used backing up other solos. Place the bow at the bouncing point (near the middle) and use as little amount of bow as possible. Relax, and don't be concerned about making the bow bounce. For a special effect play very near the bridge (sul ponticello). (The piano accompaniment to Careless Love may be used.)

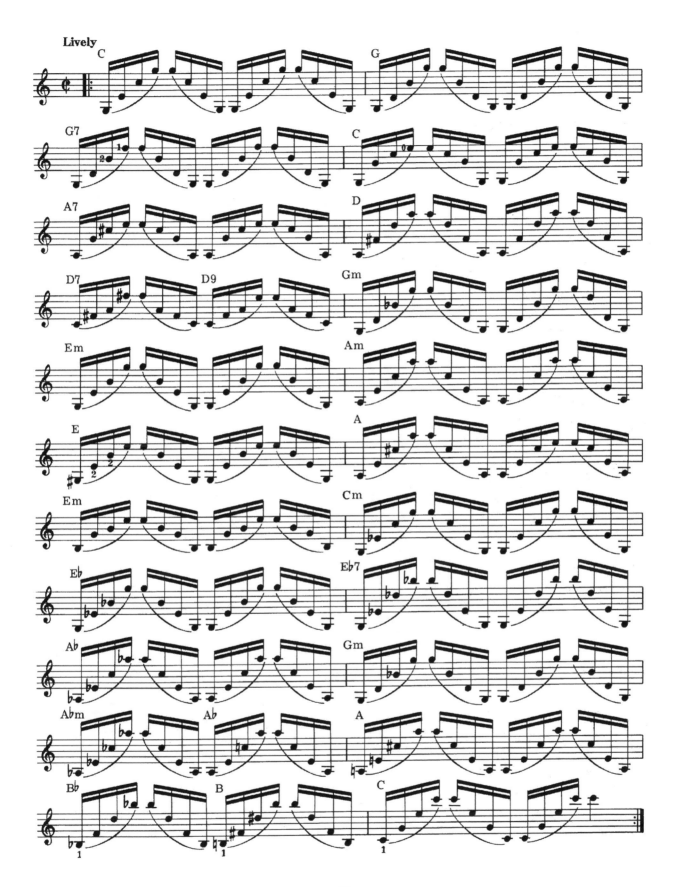

73

Very lively

TREMOLO BOWINGS

There are two types of tremolo bowing, measured and unmeasured. Measured tremolo means a definite number of notes are heard in each beat, indicated by the number of lines through the stem of the note. See (1). Unmeasured tremolo means no definite number of notes will be played. The player moves the bow back and forth as rapidly as possible, usually in the upper part of the bow. This is indicated by three lines through the stem of the note. See (2). There is also a type of tremolo called fingered tremolo, or slurred tremolo. See (3). This is an unmeasured type of tremolo and may be used on single notes or on double stops. It may be used effectively at the ends of tunes which end in the keys of G, D, or A, and others. See the examples in (4).

Measured Tremolo

77

SHUFFLE BOWINGS

Shuffle bowings are useful both in backing up others and as occasional solo use. There are many variations of the shuffle bowings. They are used primarily by jazz and bluegrass fiddlers.

These bowings may be used on adjacent strings using single notes (see examples 1 and 2), but they often use double stops (see example 3).

Two of the characteristics of shuffle bowings are the string crossings and the use of accents, which are very important. The following shuffle bowings are most effective in fast tempos.

(two measure changes)

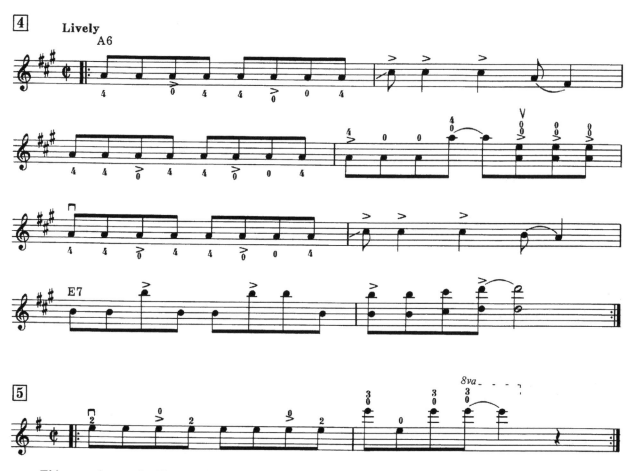

This may be used with any chord containing an E, such as C6, A7, E7.

Practice Slowly at First

83

STACCATO BOWINGS

There are many special types of bowings, most of which are not used in jazz performance, but there are a few, including two of the on the string types which have occasional use. They are the group staccato and the martele. The group staccato notes are slurred together and each note begins with a little "bite", and is then detached from the note which follows. This is indicated with a dot placed under or over the head of the note. See (1). The same is true of the martele , except each note takes a separate stroke. See (2). The fiddle tune "Old Joe Clark" will be used to illustrate these bowings and others.

OLD JOE CLARK

84

The violin may occasionally take a rhythmic part by playing staccato down bow afterbeats.

[1] Examples of jete (thrown) bowing, done in the upper part of the bow.

OLD JOE CLARK

VARIATIONS

Four selections are used here. The first three are based on folk tunes. The fourth was written by the author.

"Frankie and Johnny," "Careless Love," and "Every Night When the Sun Goes In," present variations written by the author, but the last variation in each tune is only partially written. You should complete this variation by improvising a part for the measures which are not completed. It is suggested that you try this with your violin, using half notes or quarter notes at first, if you need to. If you are satisfied with what you have played, then it is suggested that you try improvising the whole tune. It will help if you have an accompaniment. Don't be discouraged. It may take many attempts before you are able to improvise as you would like to. Your talent, your musical background and your persistence are all important in being able to improvise. If you are not satisfied with the way your improvisation turns out it is suggested that you write your own ideas in the measures which are not completed. Remember that in addition to the tones around which the melody and harmony are "centered" you may also use non-chord tones. Your ear will have to be the final authority.

A fourth tune, composed by the author, is included. The first part, titled "Sweet and Sour," is a moderately slow melody based on simple chords in the key of C. Part two, called "Sweet and Sour Jam," presents an outline of the same chords used in part one, but in a faster tempo, with the intent that the player will improvise his own music, or will write his own variations, "centering" his music around the chord tones which are given.

FRANKIE AND JOHNNY
(With Variations)

arr. by Usher Abell

Melody

*Fill in your own ideas

FRANKIE AND JOHNNY

arr. by Usher Abell

CARELESS LOVE

arr. by Usher Abell

*Fill in with your own ideas

CARELESS LOVE

arr. by Usher Abell

94

EVERY NIGHT WHEN THE SUN GOES IN
(with Variations)

arr.by Usher Abell

C.

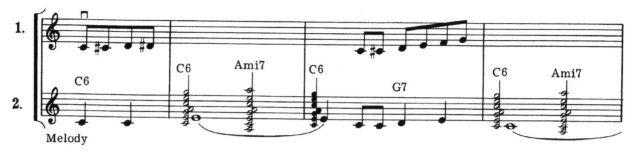

Melody

* Fill in with your own ideas.

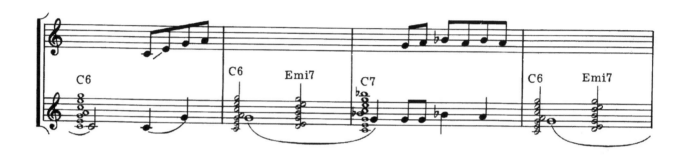

EVERY NIGHT WHEN THE SUN GOES IN

97

SWEET AND SOUR

Violin

by Usher Abell

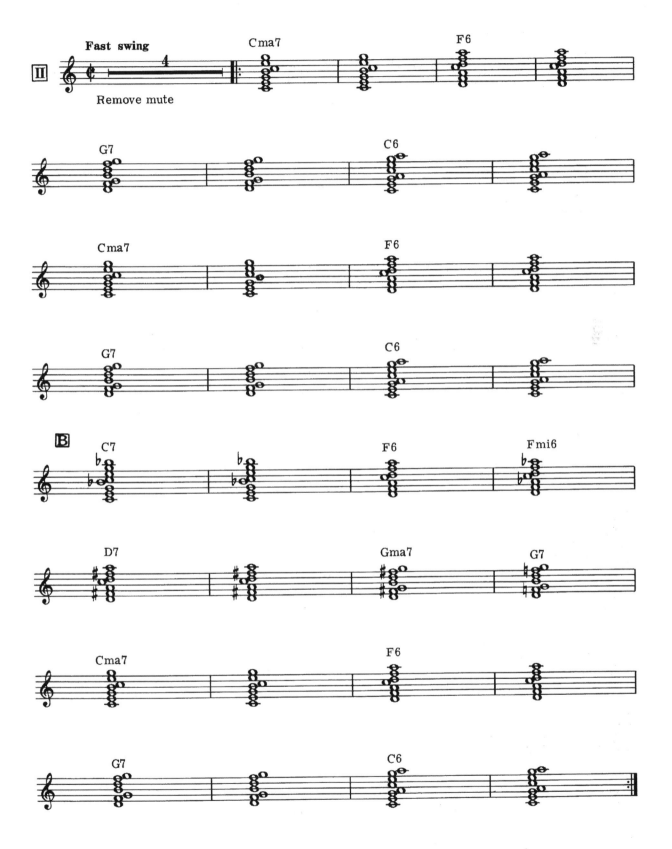

SWEET AND SOUR

by Usher Abell

SWEET AND SOUR JAM

SIXTEEN JAZZ VIOLIN PIECES
AND STUDIES
By Usher Abell

The majority of these are written out in 16 measures, some in AABA form, and based on commonly used harmonic progressions.

Numbers 1-3-5-6-8-10-12-15-16 use jazz styles.

Numbers 2-4-7-9-14 are ballad types. Number 7 is based on the two pentatonic scales, D and A. The eighth note figures may be played <u>as</u> <u>written</u> or in jazz style.

Number 11 is built on a blues pattern using the Key of B♭ for the first 12 measures and F for the second 12 measures.

Number 13 is also based on a blues pattern but is in a fast tempo. There are four 12 measure sections. They can be played separately, or all sections can be played, and then repeated, to make a more extended piece.

Number 12 is centered around one chord, the D9 chord, but also using some non-chord tones. The accompaniment, if one is used, should be inventive, especially by using inversions of the D9 chord.

104

107

109

* Fingered tremolo and downward slide.

112

RECORDINGS FEATURING
JAZZ VIOLIN PLAYERS

Stephane Grappelli
Everest FS311

Stephane Grappelli and Gary Burton
Paris Encounter SD1597

Stephane Grappelli
Young Django PAUSA 7041

Stephane Grappelli
Satin Doll Vanguard VSD81/82

Stephane Grappelli
Homage to Django Classic Jazz 23

Stephane Grappelli
Afternoon in Paris Pausa 7071

Stuff Smith
Everest FS238

Stuff Smith
Memorial Album Prestige 7691

Stuff Smith (with Asmussen, Grappelli and Ponty)
Violin Summit
EMIMPS5C06461227

Joe Venuti and Marian McPartland
The Maestro and Friend Halcyon 112

Joe Venuti and George Barnes
Gems Concord Jazz 14

Joe Venuti and George Barnes
Live at the Concord Summer Festival
Concord Jazz 30

Joe Venuti and his Big Band
Golden Era Records LP 1506(1)

Joe Venuti and Eddie Lang
Stringing the Blues Columbia CL1926
(recorded during the twenties and thirties)

Other jazz recordings are listed in the Schwann Record Catalogs.

ARRANGEMENTS BASED ON
THREE WELL KNOWN TUNES

Variations on three well known tunes are presented: "Oh,

When the Saints Come Marching In," "Just a Closer Walk With

Thee," and "Mother Doesn't Allow Any Fiddle Playing in Here"

(based on Mama Don't 'Low no Music Playing in Here). These are

written for violin with an easy piano accompaniment. Also, the

chords are indicated in the violin part so that the player may see

how the music is "centered" around the chords. The performer is

encouraged to make any changes, by improvising or by writing

his own "licks." These three tunes also include an optional second

violin part.

Many of the "licks," bowings and techniques used in these

selections are included in the Jazz Violin Studies.

OH, WHEN THE SAINTS GO MARCHING IN

1st Violin

arr. by Usher Abell

OH, WHEN THE SAINTS GO MARCHING IN

arr. by Usher Abell

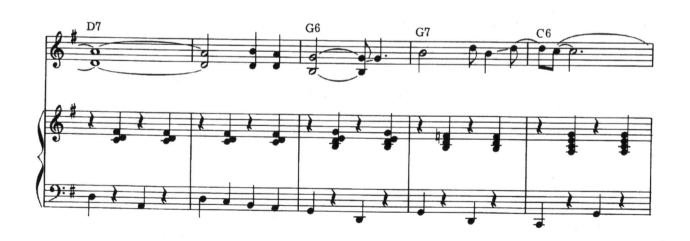

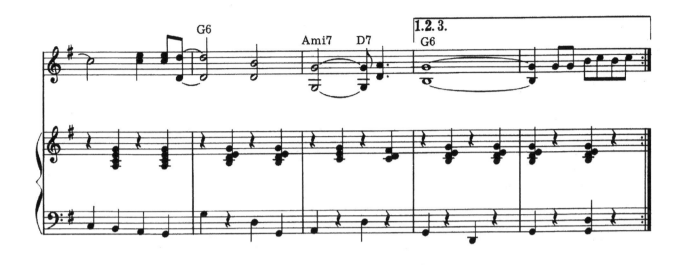

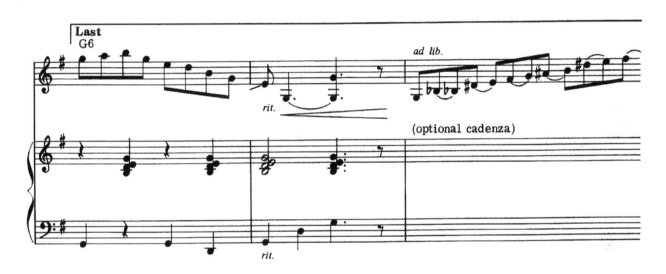

119

OH, WHEN THE SAINTS GO MARCHING IN

2nd Violin

arr. by Usher Abell

120

JUST A CLOSER WALK WITH THEE

1st Violin

arr. by Usher Abell

* Fingered tremolo.

JUST A CLOSER WALK WITH THEE

arr. by Usher Abell

play 3 times

125

126

JUST A CLOSER WALK WITH THEE

2nd Violin

arr. by Usher Abell

129

MOTHER DOESN'T ALLOW ANY
FIDDLE PLAYING IN HERE

1st Violin

arr. by Usher Abell

131

optional ending

MOTHER DOESN'T ALLOW ANY
FIDDLE PLAYING IN HERE

arr. by Usher Abell

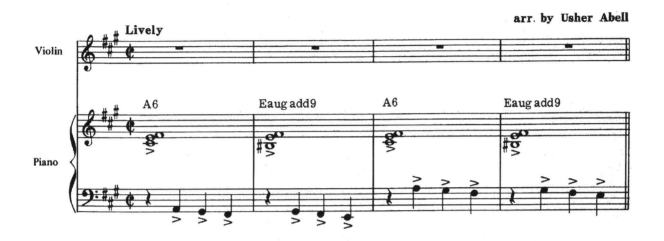

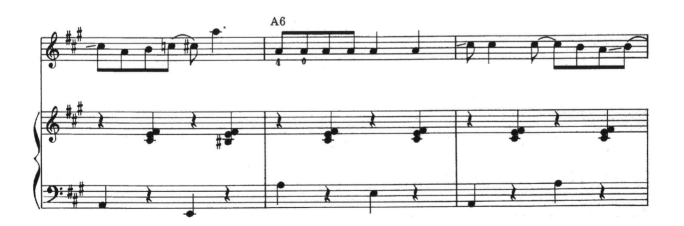

optional ending

134

MOTHER DOESN'T ALLOW ANY
FIDDLE PLAYING IN HERE

2nd Violin

arr. by Usher Abell

FIDDLER'S FOLLY

by Usher Abell

137

Note: ① all eight note are played as triplets, 𝄾𝄽𝄻 𝄾𝄽𝄻 etc.

② ⌣ before a note indicates a slide into it.

③ Variety may be acheived by violinist or pianist improvising once or more between
   B and C .

④ Violinist may play from A to B alone.

FIDDLER'S FOLLY

by Usher Abell

139

To Ken Putnam
SEQUEL

Violin

by Usher Abell

143

SEQUEL

by Usher Abell

145

WILD BIRD

Violin

by Usher Abell

148

WILD BIRD

by Usher Abell

SOME RECOMMENDED BOOKS
RELATED TO JAZZ, STRING PLAYING
AND MUSIC FUNDAMENTALS

Anthology of Fiddle Styles by David Reiner (Mel Bay
Publications, Inc., Pacific, Mo.).

Anthology of Jazz Violin Styles by Dave Reiner and Glen Asch
(1982, Mel Bay Publications, Inc., Pacific, Mo.)

Basic Music Skills by Leon Dallin (1971, Wm. C. Brown Co.,
Dubuque, Iowa)

Basic Studies in Music by William H. Barter, Jr. (1968,
Allyn and Bacon, Boston).

Blues Fiddle by Julie Lyonn Lieberman (1982, Mel Bay
Publications, Inc., Pacific, Mo.)

Chord Construction and Analysis, Elements of Jazz and Pop, by Ray
Cassarinno (1978, Consolidated Music Publishers, N.Y.)

It's Time for Some Piano Changes by Dick Hyman and Clem
DeRosa (1980, Kendor Music, Inc., Delevan, N.Y.).

Jazz Improvisation Method for Violin and Viola by David
Baker (1976, Maher Publications, Chicago).

Jazz Styles by Mark C. Gridley (1989, Prentice Hall, Inc.,
Englewood Cliffs, N.J.).

Jazz Violin by Matt Glaser and Stephane Grappelli (1981,
Oak Publications, N.Y., N.Y.).

Practical Beginning Theory by Bruce Benward and Barbara
Garvey Seagrave (1966, Wm. C. Brown Co., Dubuque, Iowa)

Solo Jazz Violin by Warren Nunes and Lynne Smithwick
(1978, Charles Hansen Music and Books, Inc., N.Y., N.Y.).

Standardized Chord Symbol Notation by Carl Brandt and
Clinton Roemer (1976, Roerick Music Co., Sherman Oaks, Ca.).

The Technique of Orchestration by Kent Kennan (1970,
Prentice Hall, Inc., Englewood Cliffs, N.J.).

Workbook in the Fundamentals of Music by H. Owen Reed
(1949, Mills Music, Inc., N.Y., N.Y.).

Made in the USA
Middletown, DE
02 September 2019